W9-ANB-148

THE HOLOCAUST
THE DEATH CAMPS

Sean Sheehan

RAINTREE
STECK-VAUGHN
RSVP PUBLISHERS

A Harcourt Company

Austin   New York
www.raintreesteckvaughn.com

Published by Raintree Steck-Vaughn Publishers,
an imprint of Steck-Vaughn Company

Library of Congress Cataloging-in-Publication Data
Sheehan, Sean, 1951-
  The death camps / Sean Sheehan.
     p. cm. -- (The Holocaust)
  Originally published : London : Hodder Children's Books, 2000.
  Includes bibliographical references and index.
  ISBN 0-7398-3258-1
  1. World War, 1939–1945--Concentration camps--Juvenile literature. 2. Holocaust, Jewish (1939–1945)--Juvenile literature. [1. Concentration camps. 2. Holocaust, Jewish (1939–1945).] I. Title. II. Series.

D804.34 .S53   2001
943.53'18—dc21   00-055247

Printed in Italy. Bound in the United States.
1 2 3 4 5 6 7 8 9 0 05 04 03 02 01

Cover photos: The perimeter fence at the Auschwitz death camp in Poland; Holocaust survivors stare out from behind the death camp walls.

Page 1: A sign in Polish and German warns outsiders away from the electrified fence of Auschwitz death camp. Many prisoners died on this fence in a desperate attempt to escape or to deliberately put an end to their suffering.

Picture Acknowledgments

AKG 5, 8 (bottom), 11, 14, 15, 16, 18 (top & bottom), 20, 21, 22 (left – Michael Teller), 34, 37, 45, 47, 50, 52, 56; Aspect Pictures 22–3 (right), 25; Camera Press cover (background photo), 1, 4, 6, 8 (top), 9, 13, 33, 35, 39, 40, 42, 51, 53; Moshe Galili 57; Hodder Wayland Picture Library 24 (Wiener Library), 27 (Imperial War Museum), 29 (Wiener Library), 58 (Imperial War Museum); Hulton-Getty Picture Collection: cover (main photo); Peter Newark Pictures 7; Chris Shwarz 10, 19, 26, 31, 32, 36, 41, 55; Topham Picturepoint 43; United States Holocaust Memorial Museum (USHMM) 12, 17, 28, 30, 38, 42, 44, 46, 46, 49, 54, 59.

CONTENTS

The Beginnings of the Death Camps 4

How the Camps Worked 12

The Mechanics of Mass Murder 22

Daily Life and Daily Death 32

People in the Camps 42

The End of the Camps 52

Dateline 60

Resources 61

Glossary 62

Index 64

THE BEGINNINGS OF THE DEATH CAMPS

Nazism

BETWEEN 1941 and 1945, during World War II, about six million Jews were murdered by the Nazis and their allies in occupied Europe. This is what is meant by the term Holocaust.

"Nazi" is a term used to designate the National German Socialist Worker's Party and its members. The head of the Nazi party and, since 1933, the leader of Germany was Adolf Hitler. Hitler's plan was to establish a new German empire by conquering and enslaving the "inferior" Slavic people to Germany's east. This new Germany would be dedicated to the idea of "racial purity." To Hitler and the Nazis, the greatest threat to Germany's racial purity were Europe's Jews.

Soon after Hitler came to power in January 1933, the Nazis established a system of concentration camps across Germany. At first, the prisoners in these camps were political opponents of the Nazis, especially communists and socialists. By 1941, these camps held 75,000 prisoners. A large percentage of these prisoners were Jews.

Left: On April 20, 1941, Hitler celebrated his 52nd birthday. In the same year, plans were made for the extermination of Jews in Nazi-occupied Europe.

Left: A Jewish family from Amsterdam prepares for deportation in the summer of 1943. The belongings they carried would have been taken from them on their arrival at one of the death camps in Poland.

World War II began in September 1939 when Germany invaded Poland. In June 1941, the war entered its most destructive phase with Germany's invasion of the Soviet Union. With the war against the Soviet Union came the Nazis' decision to undertake what they called the "final solution" to the Jewish problem—the murder of all Jews under their control. In occupied Poland, six death camps were built.

Concentration and Labor Camps

The first concentration camp was created at Dachau in Germany, in March 1933. The concentration camp system was run by the *Schutzstaffel*, or SS. The SS began as Hitler's bodyguard and grew over time to become a huge, elite force within the Nazi regime. The SS controlled the secret police and the administration of the concentration and death camps.

The last of the major concentration camps to be established before the outbreak of World War II was at Mauthausen in neighboring Austria, where German was the official language. There were many ethnic Germans, and Hitler himself came from one such Austrian family. Nazism had become very strong in the country, and in 1938 Austria accepted German rule. There were granite quarries near Mauthausen, and the prisoners were made to serve as slave labor.

Most of the camps soon functioned as labor camps. Although these camps, unlike Auschwitz and the five others in Poland, were not specifically death camps, most of the prisoners there died of exhaustion, overwork, starvation, disease, or execution. For example, an estimated two-thirds of the prisoners at Mauthausen died there.

Below: In the years leading to the outbreak of war in 1939, Joseph Goebbels, Germany's propaganda minister, was in charge of persuading the German people to support Nazi policy.

Mass Murder

The occupation of Poland in 1939, with its population of three million Jews, brought Nazism to a new level of brutality. The consequences, especially for Jews and other minorities, were shattering. Some 6 million Poles, nearly 20 percent of the population of Poland, were killed by the Germans. The whole country was subjected to a ruthless operation to remove Jews from society. All Jews were transported to specially established ghettos in Polish cities where they were confined until the Nazis began implementing their final solution. In the ghettos, as in the work camps, starvation and disease took the life of many Jews.

In 1941, after occupying much of Europe, Germany invaded Russia. Vast areas of land were occupied, and huge civilian populations, including millions of Jews, came under Nazi control. Special military forces, the *Einsatzgruppen*, had the task of seeking out and killing all those identified as enemies of the German state. In occupied territory this was the beginning of the organized killing of Jews. Millions of Jews were shot by *Einsatzgruppen* firing squads.

Below: Many Polish Jews were forced to do manual work for the Germans. At the end of a day's work, they returned to the ghettos where they were forced to live.

The *Einsatzgruppen* began with the executions of Jewish men. In August 1941 this policy was extended to Jewish women and children, too. Victims were mowed down by machine guns or shot individually—as many as 30,000 at a time—and buried in large pits that they had been forced to dig themselves.

Mauthausen

W.J. Sacks, a prisoner who survived the Mauthausen concentration camp, described work in the granite quarry:

It was notorious for the 186 steps which you had to climb at least seven times a day. And if that was not enough, an SS officer and a Kapo [a prisoner with supervisory duties] stood over us, the rocks were heavy, the sun burned our shaved heads mercilessly, and the gravel cut our bare feet. I went down with gastroenteritis, as we fell upon some cold water that had been stagnant so long it was green, and we drank it, ignoring the fact that we were being beaten on the back or pushed to the ground. I also saw the terrifying agony experienced by those dying of a twisted bowel. These wretches pleaded for death; the SS officer would laugh and say to them: "Using a bullet on you would be a waste of 18 pfennigs"; a few minutes later he would be shooting healthy people.

(Quoted in Maria Hochberg-Mariańska and Noe Grüss, *The Children Accuse*)

During the second half of 1941 it became obvious to those Nazis directing this policy that the physical task of killing many thousands of people was becoming impractical. The psychological stress placed on the executioners, as well as the problem of what to do with the inhabitants of the now horrifically overcrowded ghettos, were added factors that led to the consideration of "easier" and more "comprehensive" methods of killing.

When Heinrich Himmler, the head of the SS, visited Minsk, a city in the Soviet territory of Belarus, on an inspection tour of occupied eastern Europe, he saw executions taking place. He asked those in charge to devise other methods of killing. By the autumn of 1941, this research had led to experiments in which the poisonous exhaust from trucks was used to gas victims.

Above: Two children, wearing armbands to identify them as Jewish, return to the Warsaw ghetto.

The Death Camps

The decision to exterminate all of Europe's Jews was made sometime around the middle of 1941. Up until this time some Jews had been allowed to emigrate from Nazi-occupied Europe, but this now came to an end. The deportation of Jews to eastern Europe began in October 1941. "The Jewish Question must be resolved in the course of the war, for only so can it be solved without a worldwide outcry," stated the German Foreign Office.

Many tens of thousands of Jews had died of starvation in the ghettos and been executed in Poland and Russia. But the decision to prevent Jewish emigration from Europe and create special death camps for the murder of an entire group of people marks the beginning of the Holocaust (known as the *Shoah* in Hebrew).

Below: The death camps were built by prisoners of war, Jews, and other slave laborers.

Right: Joseph Goebbels (third from left) sits at Hitler's side. Like Hitler, Goebbels avoided being tried for his part in the war by committing suicide in 1945.

The establishment of the death camps required a great deal of planning and organization. Established German firms with good reputations were consulted regarding the design and building of the crematoriums that would have to dispose of hundreds of thousands of corpses. Much thought was given to finding the most efficient method of mass murder, with the Nazis eventually deciding to use Zyklon B, a pesticide.

In January 1942, at Lake Wannsee outside Berlin, the most important Nazi leaders—but not Hitler—met to organize the "Final Solution." According to surviving records of the conference, the Nazis decided that: "Europe is to be combed from West to East in the course of the practical implementation of the Final Solution....The evacuated Jews will first be taken, group by group, to so-called transit ghettos, in order to be transported farther east from there." As a result of the Wannsee Conference, the Jews corralled in the ghettos now found their surroundings transformed into transit camps, their destinations the recently created death camps.

On March 27, 1942, Joseph Goebbels, Hitler's minister of propaganda, praised the regime's handling of the extermination of the Jews in his diary: "No other government and no other regime would have the strength for such a global solution of the question." The fact that the solution consisted of organized mass murder was left unsaid.

A Letter from the Russian Front

From a letter by Karl Kretschmer, a member of the SS serving in Russia in 1942, to his family back in Germany:

Sunday, September 27
Dear Soska,
I am feeling wretched and am in horribly low spirits. How I'd like to be with you all . . . I must pull myself out of it. The sight of the dead (including women and children) is not very cheering. But we are fighting this war for the survival or non-survival of our people . . . As the war is in our opinion a Jewish war, the Jews are the first to feel it. Here in Russia, wherever the German soldier is, no Jew remains.

(Quoted in E. Klee, W. Dressen & V. Riess, *Those Were the Days*)

The Camp System

The extent of the camp system as a whole is astonishing. Most camps were small-scale labor camps, and at the height of World War II there were more than 10,000 in total, mostly in eastern Europe. There were about 50 concentration camps, and six death, or extermination, camps: Auschwitz, Chelmno, Belzec, Majdanek, Sobibor, and Treblinka (see map on page 13).

All the Nazi institutions for the Holocaust—concentration camps, labor camps, death camps, even the ghettos—shared basic characteristics. They were designed to confine prisoners with little or no regard for the legalities or the long-term health of the prisoners. Even in the ghettos, for example, Jews were limited to starvation rations. In all of the camps and ghettos, long-term confinement was virtually guaranteed to result in sickness and death. Indeed, it was intended to do so.

Opposite: Inmates of a concentration camp march to their work duties.

Below: The harsh climate of eastern European winters, combined with an inadequate diet and hard physical labor, killed many camp prisoners.

Chronology

1933	**January**	Hitler becomes chancellor of Germany
	March	First concentration camp established at Dachau
1935	**Spring**	Nazis organize attacks on Jews and Jewish stores
1938	**November**	Jews forbidden to visit places of entertainment and expelled from schools. Jewish businesses closed down
1939	**September**	Start of World War II; ghettos created in Poland
1941	**April**	German army high command ordered to allow SS units to operate alongside army units in Russia
	June	Germany invades Russia
	July	High-ranking Nazis begin working on the Final Solution
	September	First prisoners gassed at Auschwitz
	December	First Jews gassed at Chelmno
1942	**January**	Wannsee Conference organizes plans for the Final Solution
	March	Gassing begins at Belzec
	May	Start of large-scale gassings at Auschwitz

HOW THE CAMPS WORKED

Worked to Death

THE FIRST camps, as we have seen, were established in Germany to punish and "re-educate" political opponents of the Nazis. Within a few years, the SS began to exploit some of the concentration camps as a source of free labor by creating their own building materials industry. Buchenwald and Sachsenhausen were both close to deposits of clay and loam, which could be used to make bricks. In 1938 Himmler founded the German Earth and Stone Works to set up the operation as a profit-making business. The brick-making factory near Sachsenhausen became the largest of its kind in the world, but the wealth being produced did nothing to improve the quality of life in the camps. The opposite happened, because profits could be maximized by working the prisoners to death before replacing them with new prisoners.

An inmate of Buchenwald, who survived the harsh life of working in the loam pits, described the cost in human terms: "Every night saw its procession of dead and injured, trundled into camp on wheelbarrows and stretchers.....The mistreatment was indescribable—stonings, beatings, 'accidents,' deliberate hurlings into the pit, shooting, and every imaginable form of torture."

Below: Germans used camp prisoners to help them in the war effort. These prisoners at Buchenwald are building a railroad line to link the camp with Weimar in Germany.

The SS had grown from a small force set up to defend the Nazi party into the most powerful organization in Germany. It was able to negotiate directly with many of the large industrial companies that wanted to profit from a ready supply of cheap labor. This was a development that followed from the success of early work camps such as Mauthausen. These operations co-existed alongside a very different objective—the extermination of Europe's Jews. Orders were received from Berlin to adapt some of the work camps so that they could contribute to the task of killing people. This is how the camp at Majdanek in Poland, which started out as a concentration and labor camp for Poles and Russian prisoners, became a death camp by the end of 1941.

Right: Little remains of the Majdanek death camp. This stone carving marks where the camp entrance used to be.

Below: There were concentration camps in Germany, but the six death camps were all situated in Poland. Auschwitz's railroad connections helped make it the largest camp.

Four New Death Camps

In addition to Auschwitz and Majdanek, four other death camps were established in Poland between December 1941 and the middle of 1942. At the Chelmno death camp most Jews were executed by firing squad or in mobile gas vans. Chelmno was designed solely for executions. The only prisoners who were not killed were those selected for digging graves and burying the dead. Gassing started there in December 1941, while it was March of the next year before gassing started at the Belzec camp.

Belzec was located in a remote forest area, but a railroad line connected it to Lublin, where there was a Jewish ghetto. Belzec was made up of two areas, a reception area where Jews arrived and left their clothes and belongings and a second area where three small gas chambers were built. A 6 1/2-foot (2-m) wide path, just over 164 feet (50 m) long, connected the two camps. This became known as the "tube." Like the camp as a whole, the "tube" was enclosed by barbed wire and was the prisoners' route to their deaths. Belzec was

Below: Many of the Jews deported from the Lodz ghetto, in Poland, ended up in the Chelmno death camp, which was built near the city.

Right: This storeroom in the Majdanek camp was found when the Soviet forces entered the camp to liberate survivors. This was where the clothes of murdered Jews were sorted and sent back to Germany for distribution to German citizens.

the first camp to be equipped with permanent gas chambers. In April 1942, 100 miles (160 km) to the north of Belzec, the larger Sobibor camp opened as a death camp. Franz Stangl was appointed its commandant. After a few months he was put in charge of an even larger camp at Treblinka, 75 miles (120 km) northeast of Warsaw. In *Shoah*, a documentary film containing eyewitness testimony about the Holocaust, Franz Suchomel, a former guard at Treblinka, described how, "Woven into the barbed wire were branches of pine trees... .People couldn't see anything to the left or right. Nothing. You couldn't see through it. Impossible."

Treblinka, Belzec, and Sobibor received well over a million people—almost all Jews—who were killed as soon as they arrived at the camp. The Germans began to build Treblinka in May of 1942, and by September 250,000 Jews had been killed in Treblinka alone. There was a short delay in the autumn when larger gas chambers were constructed, but the exterminations soon resumed.

Bergen-Belsen

Bergen-Belsen was never a typical concentration camp. It was established in 1943 to house a special group of wealthy and influential Jews. The Germans thought they might be able to exchange them for Germans imprisoned by the British and Americans. The inmates of Belsen, as the camp has come to be known, had to work and survive on little food, but conditions were generally better than at any other camps and there were no gas chambers. In 1944, as the Russians began their advance into Europe, the Nazis started evacuating camps in eastern Europe. Belsen was flooded with starving evacuees from these camps, who were left there to die.

Auschwitz

In 1940 a decision was made to set up a new camp for Polish political prisoners. The place chosen was near the town of Oswiecim in southern Poland. The German name for the town, which had important rail connections with other parts of Europe, was Auschwitz. Rudolf Höss, a committed Nazi, first arrived at Auschwitz to take control of the new camp in April 1940. Thirty German criminal prisoners then arrived in May to start work building the camp. They were helped by 200 Jews rounded up from the local area.

This first camp that Höss supervised, to be known as Auschwitz I, remained largely a prison work camp for a variety of inmates, especially Jews and political prisoners. A large number of prisoners were killed there, but its primary function was as an administration center for the reception of Jews deported from all corners of Nazi-occupied Europe. The first prisoners arrived in June. Shortly after, peasants living in local villages were expelled to create more room for the camps. An area measuring 6 miles by 3 miles (9.6 by 4.8 km) became prison property.

Below: Heinrich Himmler (in uniform) examines plans for the massive I. G. Farben plant at Auschwitz with the German manufacturer Max Faust.

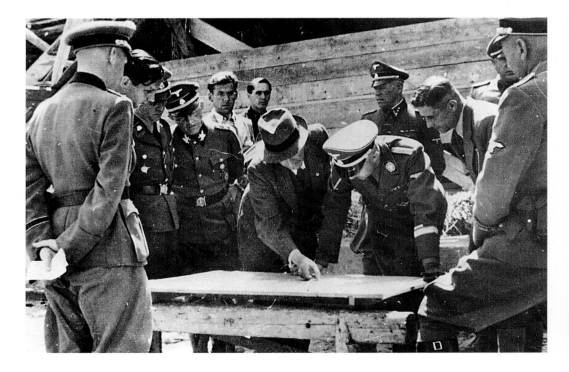

Auschwitz Facts

Guards: some 7,000 guards were employed at various times

Victims: the number of people who died at Auschwitz between 1941 and 1945 is uncertain, but the commonly accepted total figure is 1.1 million, almost 1 million of whom were Jews.

Auschwitz II:

Buildings: 200 wooden huts, each 100 feet by 30 feet (30.4 m by 9 m)

Daily population: from 30,000 to 40,000 to more than 120,000

Gas chambers: four

Capacity: in the summer of 1944 the camp staff worked 24 hours round the clock, gassing almost 500,000 Hungarian Jews in less than two months

I. G. Farben plant at Auschwitz III

Employed: about 40,000 slave laborers

Survivors: less than 15,000

AUSCHWITZ I (MAIN CAMP)
OSWIECIM, POLAND
25 AUGUST 1944

The planning of Auschwitz II began in late 1941. Building work started early the next year at a site some 2 miles (3.2 km) away on the other side of the train line, near a village called Birkenau by the Germans. Birkenau underwent considerable development in the course of its existence. In the summer of 1942, when three gas chambers capable of holding over 1,000 people were ready for operation, plans were already being made for its expansion.

Above: This aerial photograph of Auschwitz I was one of many taken by Allied planes secretly between April 1944 and January 1945.

Auschwitz III was established at the nearby village of Monowitz. By the middle of 1942 it served as a slave-labor camp for the huge German chemical company, I. G. Farben, which was one of several German companies that used slave labor at Auschwitz. The laborers were mostly Jewish. Some were also forced to work as miners in two local coal mines that were taken over by I. G. Farben.

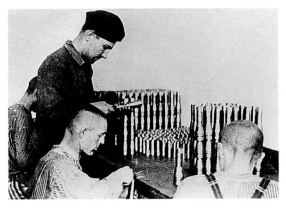

In addition to the main Auschwitz sites, 50 smaller satellite camps were dotted around the area. They also employed slave labor. These included a cement plant, a steel factory, a shoe factory, and a specialized camp where fuses were removed from unexploded bombs dropped by the Allies in bombing raids over Germany. Auschwitz is the common name given to the three main camps as well as the various satellite camps.

Above: A German supervisor oversees slave laborers working in a munitions factory.

Below: Himmler inspects work on the I. G. Farben plant at Auschwitz in July 1942.

Above: "Work Makes You Free" is the translation of the German words above the main gate at Auschwitz.

In July of 1942 Himmler made an inspection of the Auschwitz camps to ensure that everything was going according to plan. He observed the process of killing, from when Jews first got off the trains up to the moment of their death. "He made no remark regarding the process of extermination but remained quite silent," remembered Höss, the camp's commandant. Before he left the following day, Himmler announced that he was satisfied with the camp's operation.

It was Höss who came up with the infamous slogan that hung above the main gate at Auschwitz. *Arbeit Macht Frei*, read the German phrase: "Work Makes You Free."

Who Made the Camps Work?

On a day-to-day level, thousands of people had to be involved to make the camps work. The extent to which ordinary Germans knew about the Holocaust is a matter of debate. Historian Daniel Goldhagen, the author of a controversial study, *Hitler's Willing Executioners*, claims that most Germans supported the policy of mass murder, and that between 100,000 and 500,000 Germans were directly involved in the Holocaust. Other historians dispute this interpretation, arguing that the SS tried to hide the truth from ordinary Germans and that the majority did not support the mass murder of Jews and perhaps even did not know the scale of what was happening.

Holocaust Bonanza

"Holocaust Bonanza" is a deliberately offensive term that has been used by historians to describe the way in which both German and other international companies used slave labor from the concentration and death camps to increase their profits. More than 90 companies used slave labor at Buchenwald, and 52 companies used Dachau. Fifty-one companies, including the Ford motor company's German operation, used slave labor from Auschwitz.

The I. G. Farben company, serviced by slave labor at Auschwitz, set up plants there to produce synthetic rubber and convert coal into oil. Those who ran I. G. Farben were businessmen, not necessarily Nazis. They saw the opportunity to increase their profits by entering into a commercial arrangement with the SS, whom they paid for an unlimited supply of cheap labor. The rate was the equivalent of $1.00 a day for a skilled worker, 75 cents a day for unskilled labor and, toward the end of the war, 40 cents for a child laborer. No money went to the prisoners, one of whom drew a comparison between his existence and that of the slaves of the ancient world: "Only now do I realize what price was paid for building ancient civilizations….How much blood must have poured onto the Roman roads, the bulwarks, and the city walls." To be fair to the Romans, they did place some value on their slaves. But the Germans placed no value on the Jewish laborers in camps like Auschwitz III, and worked them to death. A subsidiary company of I.G. Farben manufactured Zyklon B for the death camps.

Below: Anti-Semitic cartoons, like this one from 1936, were used by the Nazis to justify their treatment of the Jews and make ordinary Germans feel that the Jews posed a threat to their way of life.

Left: Inmates of the Dachau camp in Germany were forced to work for the German war effort.

A Policeman's Excuse

We had been drilled in such a way that we viewed all orders issued by the head of state as lawful and correct. We police went by the phrase, "Whatever serves the state is right, whatever harms the state is wrong." I would also like to say that it never entered my head that these orders could be wrong. Although I am aware that it is the duty of the police to protect the innocent, I was however at that time convinced that the Jewish people were not innocent but guilty....The thought that one should oppose or evade the order to take part in the extermination of the Jews never entered my head either. I followed these orders because they came from the highest leaders of the state and not because I was in any way afraid.

Kurt Möbius, a policeman who served in Chelmno, testifying on November 8, 1961. (Quoted in E. Klee, W. Dressen & V. Riess, *Those Were the Days*)

THE MECHANICS OF MASS MURDER

Murder by Gas

D EATH by gas was first used for killing patients in hospitals and mental asylums after the start of World War II. Fake shower rooms were built in asylums, holding about 50 inmates, and carbon-monoxide gas was piped into them. Breakdowns in the machinery were common occurrences. Because these institutions existed in German towns with residential populations, there was also the problem of disposing of corpses without drawing attention to what was happening.

The next stage was the development of gas vans. German technicians devised a method of channeling a vehicle's poisonous exhaust fumes back into its airtight interior. In theory, all the prisoners inside a van would be gassed while the vehicle drove to a burial pit in the countryside. However, there were technical problems, and sometimes there were still people gasping for air when the doors were opened. Sobibor, Belzec, and Treblinka used diesel engines to supply the gas chambers with exhaust fumes.

In the summer of 1941, Höss, the commandant of Auschwitz, was summoned to Berlin, where he personally received orders from Himmler to implement the systematic extermination of

Below left: A gas chamber reconstructed at Auschwitz I by the Polish authorities in 1948.

Below: Mass graves were dug and filled with the bodies of victims. Such graves were usually built close to death or concentration camps.

Jews in his camp. Auschwitz had been chosen, he was told, because of its size and isolation. Höss then visited other camps in Poland to assess how they gassed their prisoners. He was looking for a method of killing to suit his camp. At Chelmno he learned about the gas vans, the technical problem of distributing the gas evenly, and the fact that relatively small numbers of prisoners could be killed by this method.

Zyklon B, the trade name for a form of cyanide known as hydrocyanic acid, had been used in Auschwitz to exterminate rats and other vermin and as a disinfectant. It was so effective that Höss's deputy, Karl Fritzsch, decided to experiment with it on a group of 600 Soviet prisoners and hospital patients in September 1941. He discovered that Zyklon B proved as effective in killing people as it did rats. It also killed people very quickly, which meant more Jews could be killed in a day. This became the preferred method of extermination at Auschwitz.

The Language of Murder

At first, gas vans proved unsatisfactory because the van's large space meant that when it was filled with prisoners (referred to as "merchandise" below) the vehicle's stability was affected by the heavy weight. A German engineer proposed reducing the size of the van's capacity. In this memorandum he deals with a possible technical problem:

The manufacturers told us during a discussion that reducing the size of the van's rear would throw it badly off balance. The front axle, they claim, would be overloaded. In fact, the balance is automatically restored, because the merchandise aboard displays during the operation a natural tendency to rush to the rear doors, and is mainly found lying there at the end of the operation. So the front axle is not overloaded.

(Quoted in Ronnie S. Landau, *Studying the Holocaust*)

The Process of Mass Murder

Jews were gassed at all the death camps, but the process of mass murder at Auschwitz is better documented than at any of the other camps. The largest of all the camps, Auschwitz was the camp where the greatest number of Jews were murdered. In addition to almost 1 million Jews, 75,000 Poles, 20,000 Gypsies, and 15,000 Soviet prisoners died at Auschwitz.

By the summer of 1942, freight trains loaded with Jews had arrived at Auschwitz from several regions of Poland, Slovakia, the Netherlands, Belgium, France, and Croatia. Auschwitz became a combination of giant industrial concern and killing factory. Human beings were processed for destruction as if on a production line at a factory.

Upon arrival at Auschwitz, Jews underwent what was know as "selection," in which they were designated for labor or an immediate trip to the gas chambers. After gassing, for hygienic reasons, the corpses were hosed down by men in rubber boots

Below: Most of these women and children, photographed after getting off the boxcars at Auschwitz, would have been selected to go straight to the gas chambers.

In His Own Words

Rudolf Höss, the commandant of Auschwitz, described what happened in the "shower rooms":

The door would now be quickly screwed up and the gas discharged by the waiting disinfectors through vents in the ceilings of the gas chambers, down a shaft that led to the floor. This insured the rapid distribution of the gas. It could be observed through the peepholes in the door that those who were standing nearest to the induction vents were killed at once. It can be said that about one-third died straightaway. The remainder staggered about and began to scream and struggle for air. The screaming, however, soon changed to the death rattle and in a few minutes all lay still....The door was opened half an hour after the induction of the gas, and the ventilation switched on.

(Quoted in Jadwiga Bezwińska and Danuta Czech (eds), *KL Auschwitz*)

Above: Parts of an original furnace were used in the reconstruction of this crematorium at Auschwitz.

wielding powerful hoses. The bodies were then removed and taken to crematoriums, where they were burned. The ovens had to be stoked up before cremation and hurriedly cleaned out afterward, because there where always more corpses. Höss described the problem at Auschwitz: "Depending on the size of the bodies, up to three corpses could be put into one oven at the same time. The time required for cremation....took twenty minutes." At this pace sometimes the system became overloaded, and there were delays caused by the failure of the crematoriums, which just could not keep up with the numbers of Jews sent to Auschwitz.

Streamlining Murder

Mass murder at the camps was treated like an industrial process, one that would benefit from being organized in the most efficient way possible. Bearing this in mind, the Germans tried not to let the victims know what was going to happen to them. They were already frightened by the experience of being rounded up and herded like cattle onto trains. When the organized roundup of Jews from German-occupied Europe began in early 1942, victims were told they were being resettled in eastern Europe. To help convince them this was the case, the Germans told them to bring their belongings and valuables with them for their new life.

In memoirs and interviews, Germans who worked in the death camps have told of the efforts that were made to deceive Jews into thinking they were not about to be murdered. Most often, new arrivals were told that the large windowless cells into which they were herded—the gas chambers—were showers where they could wash before being assigned living quarters. At Sobibor, one of the SS leaders wore a white doctor's coat to reinforce the impression that the showers served a hygienic purpose. At Treblinka, the commandant had a fake train station constructed, complete with a painted clock and signs pointing to other destinations in Poland, to convince prisoners they had arrived

Below: Once the owners of these suitcases arrived at Auschwitz, they were never to see their possessions again. Some of the massive piles of goods discovered by the Russians liberators of the camp now form part of the exhibition for visitors to Auschwitz I.

only at a transit camp. Pots of geraniums were placed to give a reassuring sense of normality.

Such tactics were very successful in Treblinka. As a result, only about 20 SS soldiers and 80 Ukrainians were needed to carry out the killing. At Auschwitz the large "changing rooms," which could hold up to 1,000 people, had signs placed in various languages reading "Baths and Disinfecting Rooms" and instructions that shoes were to be tied together by their laces. Numbered pegs and coat hangers on the walls added to the illusion.

Attempts at deception did not always work, and of course many people knew what was about to happen to them. Some people panicked, some tried to resist, and many made efforts to comfort their children and act as normally as possible in an attempt to dignify their final moments together.

Above: This photograph of a liberated concentration camp in 1945 shows the dazed survivors surrounded by their dead companions.

Pigtail

A visitor to the Auschwitz museum wrote about a display case with a huge pile of human hair found in a store room in 1945:

When all the women in the transport
had their heads shaved
four workmen with brooms made of
birch twigs swept up
and gathered up the hair

Behind clean glass
the stiff hair lies
of those suffocated in gas chambers
there are pins and side combs
in this hair

The hair is not shot through with light
is not parted by the breeze
is not touched by any hand
or rain or lips

In huge chests
clouds of dry hair
of those suffocated
and a faded plait
a pigtail with a ribbon
pulled at school
by naughty boys.

(*Pigtail* by Tadeusz Rözewicz. Quoted in Hilda Schiff, *Holocaust Poetry*)

Left: This crate of wedding rings was discovered by American troops when they searched a cave adjoining the Buchenwald concentration camp.

The Spoils of Murder

Part of the system of streamlining mass murder involved trying to make sure that absolutely nothing of any commercial value went to waste. Everyone, whether selected to work or to die, was stripped of belongings upon arrival at a camp. Prisoners carried their most precious and essential belongings with them, so there was a vast amount of valuable goods that the German authorities expected to be sent to Berlin for processing. The process did not end with death. Before they were taken to the crematoriums, the corpses of gassed Jews were checked for gold teeth, which were removed and collected in a bucket containing acid that would melt away flesh and bone. A Jewish doctor at Auschwitz calculated that, at the peak of its operation, up to 20 pounds (9 kg) of gold could be collected over a period of 24 hours. The long hair of females was cut off and collected for various purposes, including stuffing pillows and making socks for U-boat (submarine) crews.

A Jewish prisoner who was forced to work in the crematoriums spoke in the film *Shoah* of how, "The Germans even forbade us to us the words 'corpse' or 'victim' . . . . The Germans made us refer to the bodies as *figuren*, that is, as puppets, as dolls, or as *schmattes*, which means 'rags.'"

It Was my Job to Shoot These People

From a statement of Will Mentz, known as "the gunman" of Treblinka:

There were always some ill and frail people on the transports . . . . These people would be taken to the hospital area and stood or laid down at the edge of the grave. When no more ill or wounded were expected it was my job to shoot these people. I did this by shooting them in the neck with a 9-mm pistol. They then collapsed or fell to one side and were carried down into the grave by the two hospital work-Jews. The bodies were sprinkled with chlorinated lime.

(Quoted in Claude Lanzmann, *Shoah: The Complete Text of the Acclaimed Holocaust Film*)

Below: On arrival at Auschwitz, these Hungarian women had their heads shaved and were given thin uniforms to wear. They were separated from their families and left to wonder about their fate.

Genocide at All Costs

By 1944 the war had turned against Germany. To the west, a huge U.S. and British invasion of northern France was imminent. To the east, Soviet forces were beginning to push the Germans back from Eastern Europe.

The prospect of military defeat did not cause the Germans to divert precious resources and manpower from the Final Solution. Indeed, Auschwitz was renovated to make more efficient killing of larger numbers of Jews possible.

After invading Hungary in March 1944, the Nazis were determined to exterminate that country's entire population of Jews, who then numbered about 800,000. By this point, the Nazis needed every train available to transport their retreating troops from the Soviet Union. Even so, they used valuable fuel and trains to move Hungary's Jews from the ghettos where they had been confined to the death camps. The machinery of murder worked overtime to bring some 400,000 Hungarian Jews to Auschwitz over a period of eight weeks. Adolf Eichmann, the SS bureaucrat responsible for managing much of the final solution, briefly considered another "use" for Hungary's Jews. He offered

Below: Prisoners at Buchenwald camp are lined up in a nearby forest, awaiting execution.

to trade Jews to the British for Jeeps and trucks. The British refused the offer.

Below: These bouquets of flowers were left by visitors to the Wall of Tears at Auschwitz, where many prisoners were shot.

I Keep Forgetting

I keep forgetting
the facts and statistics
and each time
I need to know them

I look up books
these books line
twelve shelves
in my room

I know where to go
to confirm the fact
that in the Warsaw ghetto
there were 7.2 people per room . . .

and how many
bodies they crammed
in Auschwitz
at the peak of production

twelve thousand a day
I have to check
and re-check . . .

and did I dream
that at 4pm on the 19th January
58,000 emaciated inmates
were marched out of Auschwitz

. . . I can remember
people's conversations
and what someone's wife
said to someone else's husband

what a good memory
you have
people tell me.

(I Keep Forgetting by Lily Brett, quoted from Hilda Schiff *Holocaust Poetry)*

DAILY LIFE AND DAILY DEATH

Selection

F OR MOST prisoners, the crashing sound of boxcar doors being opened signaled their arrival at a death camp. Even after days spent cooped up in a sealed compartment, in which many had already died from exhaustion and suffocation, the moment of arrival brought, at most, only short-lived relief for the new arrivals. SS men in black uniforms barked orders and herded them into line. Experienced guards maintained an air of brisk efficiency. Anxious questions from terrified new arrivals were met with reassuring lies and promises. The guards tried to maintain as calm an atmosphere as possible. As one woman survivor recalled: "This is the greatest strength of the whole crime, its unbelievability. When we came to Auschwitz, we smelt the sweet smell. They [other inmates] said to us, 'There the people are gassed, three kilometers over there.' We didn't believe it."

Below: On arrival at Auschwitz II, the inmates who escaped the initial selection were separated from their friends and families, shaved, stripped of all possessions, and tattooed with a number.

The first procedure at a death camp usually occurred as soon as the prisoners were off the train. Two SS doctors waved each individual to the left—the gas chamber—or to the right, which meant, for a while at least, work and life. Age and sex were the most immediate determining factors in the selection. Women, children, and men over 40 were most often selected for death. The sick and the weak were also sent to the chambers. For those selected for work, their reprieve was only temporary. As they became sick and exhausted, they became more likely candidates for the chambers in future selections.

Below: This woman in the Bergen-Belsen concentration camp has typhus. The illness and suffering she has endured have aged her considerably.

Silent as an Aquarium

In 1943 the 25-year-old Primo Levi, an Italian Jew, was deported from Turin to Auschwitz. He describes his arrival at the camp:

A vast platform appeared before us, lit up by reflectors. A little beyond it, a row of trucks. Then everything was silent again. Someone translated: we had to climb down with our luggage and deposit it alongside the train.... A dozen SS men stood around, legs akimbo, with an indifferent air. At a certain moment they moved amongst us, and in a subdued tone of voice, with faces of stone, began to interrogate us rapidly, one by one, in bad Italian. They did not interrogate everybody, only a few: "How old? Healthy or ill?" And on the basis of the reply they pointed in two different directions. Everything was as silent as an aquarium, or as in certain dream sequences. We had expected something more apocalyptic: they seemed simple police agents. It was disconcerting and disarming.

(Quoted from Primo Levi, *Survival in Auschwitz*)

Processing

Even in an extermination camp such as Chelmno, where less than 10 of the estimated 300,000 Jews transported there are known to have survived, there was still a need to keep some people alive for essential work duties. At Auschwitz, those who were not immediately selected for gassing were ordered to strip. Their hair was shaved, and blue-and-white striped clothing was handed out to them, along with wooden clogs.

Men and women were divided before being lined up in alphabetical order so that they could be registered and tattooed on the forearm with a number. The numbering system was used to organize the daily allowances of bread and soup, and inmates who survived long enough learned to interpret the numbers: those below 80,000, for example, represented early arrivals from the Polish ghettos. As well as the tattoo, inmates received a colored triangle on their clothing to signify their status. Political prisoners had a red triangle; criminals, a green one; and homosexuals, a pink one. Jews who also fell into one of these categories were assigned a yellow triangle that went atop the other to form a Star of David, a symbol of the Jewish people.

Below: Roll call took place twice a day. This photograph records a roll call at Sachsenhausen.

haftigkeit   Opfersinn   und

Left: A camp survivor shows her tattooed number. She is wearing the Star of David in memory of those who died in the camps.

"From Now on You're Sixteen"

Elli Friedmann was 13 when she arrived at Auschwitz from Hungary with her mother, brother, and aunt. Elli, who was not aware that anyone under the age of 16 was destined for the gas chambers, remembered a noisier scene than did Primo Levi (see page 33):

The column of women, infants and children begins to move. Dogs snarl, SS men scream orders, children cry, women weep goodbyes to departing men, and I struggle with my convulsive stomach . . . He [the man making the selection] looks at me with friendly eyes. "Goldenes haar!" he exclaims and takes one of my long plaits into his hand. I am not certain I heard right. Did he say 'golden hair' about my plaits?

"Bist du Jüdin?" Are you Jewish?
The question startles me. "Yes, I am Jewish."
"Wie alt bist du?" How old are you?
"I am thirteen."
"You are tall for your age. Is this your mother?" He touches Mummy lightly on the shoulder.
"You go with your mother."
With his riding stick he parts Aunt Serena from Mummy's embrace and gently shoves Mummy and me to the group moving to the right.
"Go. And remember, from now on you're sixteen."

(Quoted in Livia Bitton-Jackson, *I Have Lived a Thousand Years*)

Daily Routine

A prisoner's day always began with a roll call before dawn. The process could take hours. Everyone was counted; even those who died during the night were propped up in position for the roll call. Then prisoners marched away to their work duties. At Auschwitz, a camp band played marching music to accompany the prisoners as they left for work each morning.

Auschwitz was largely self-sufficient, which meant that the nature of work duties varied a lot. Such places as the camp bakery provided a relatively easy work assignment, but more common was the hard labor that went into expanding buildings and laying new roads for the camp. All work, whatever its nature, was hard to bear because of the meager food allowances. Everyone was weak, and the poor food rations made disease and illness very common.

The only time that prisoners had to themselves was at night in their barracks or during the day at the latrines. Toilets usually

Below: A communal toilet at Auschwitz. Many such "facilities" in the camps were nothing more than open ditches. Lack of sanitation caused epidemics of typhus and dysentery.

consisted of a long wide ditch. Prisoners were escorted there by guards in groups of up to 50.

Death was an inescapable part of daily camp life, and prisoners did not pretend otherwise. They knew about the gas chambers, and they discussed among themselves how long it probably took to die there. They saw fellow prisoners die of disease and weakness or fall victim to the regular "selections" that weeded out those no longer capable of working. Anyone failing a selection was taken to the gas chamber and killed.

Below: In 1933, Dachau was a less deadly place than it would become after 1941.

Survival Skills

Jean Amery, a prisoner at Auschwitz, explains that educated professionals, like lawyers and teachers, often lacked the skills necessary to survive in the camp:

Camp life demanded above all bodily agility and physical courage that necessarily bordered on brutality.... Assume for a moment that we had to prevent a professional pickpocket from Warsaw from stealing our shoelaces. Circumstances permitting, an uppercut certainly helped...only very rarely did the lawyer or gymnasium teacher know how to execute an uppercut properly.... In matters of camp discipline things were also bad. Those who on the outside had practised a higher profession generally possessed little talent for bedmaking. I recall educated and cultivated comrades who, dripping with sweat, battled every morning with their straw mattress and blankets and still achieved no proper results, so that later, at the work site, they were plagued by the fear—which grew into an obsession—that on their return they would be punished with a beating or the withdrawal of food.

(Quoted from Jean Amery, *At The Mind's Limits*)

Surviving

For those not selected for immediate death, the single most important factor affecting their chance of survival was the kind of work he or she was assigned. Food rations were not enough to keep anyone alive for very long, and heavy labor, especially in the coal mines, meant certain death. Prisoners who had a trade—for example a machinist, plumber, carpenter, chemist, electrician, or cabinetmaker—stood some chance of an indoor assignment at one of the Auschwitz work camps. Businesspeople and professionals, such as lawyers or teachers, had no useful skills that could be exploited, and they were more likely to be assigned to a short life of hard labor.

Left: An early photograph taken at Sachsenhausen concentration camp. The barracks are comfortable and the food rations generous in comparison with conditions at the camp toward the end of the war.

Toward the end of 1943 there were small but significant changes in life at Auschwitz. These changes increased the chances of survival for some of those not selected for the gas chambers. The reason for this is not clear, but it may have had something to do with the growing realization that Germany was not winning the war and might ultimately be held accountable for its actions. The majority of prisoners in the Auschwitz work camps were not Jews but prisoners of war. By the middle of 1943, the decision had been made to stop gassing non-Jews. This, of course, made no difference to the fate of the Jews, who continued to arrive in large numbers.

Below: Bodies litter the sides of the road at Bergen-Belsen after its liberation in 1945.

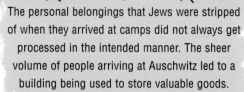

Canada

The personal belongings that Jews were stripped of when they arrived at camps did not always get processed in the intended manner. The sheer volume of people arriving at Auschwitz led to a building being used to store valuable goods. This developed into what has been called the largest black market in Europe. There was a vast trade among prisoners, kapos, and the Germans. Just about everything was for sale—food, clothes, precious stones, carpets, shoes, even the gold bars made from the teeth of victims. The barracks where the goods were stored, and pilfered from by corrupt guards, became known as Canada. Many Poles had emigrated to Canada before the war, and they had good memories of the country and its prosperity.

Surprises at Auschwitz

The idea of a hospital at Auschwitz sounds like a remarkable contradiction, but one did exist. The SS would have liked to gas everyone who was ill. They began removing patients from the hospital for executions, but the prisoners stopped seeking treatment for illness. This increased the danger of infectious diseases spreading through the camp and affecting even the guards and administrators. The result was that the hospital became something of a sanctuary, even though the SS still sometimes made selections there.

Obviously, the normal concepts of law and justice did not apply in the camps. Prisoners, however, developed their own code of justice, and certain offenses, like stealing another prisoner's food or informing on someone, were dealt with at night in secret makeshift courts. Punishments took the form of beatings or even death for serious offenses.

Astonishingly, an SS judge was sent to Auschwitz in mid-1943 to investigate corruption at the camp. An SS guard had been caught trying to send some stolen gold home to his family. The judge had already investigated financial fraud at the Buchenwald camp, where the commandant was prosecuted and executed as a result. The German military authorities were eager to uphold standards of professional conduct, yet they were carrying out

Left: Medical experiments were carried out on this dissecting table at Auschwitz.

the largest act of mass murder the world had
ever witnessed.

Auschwitz was full of macabre surprises. One was the tradition
of putting up a Christmas tree, decorated with colored lights,
close to one of the gas chambers. Most of the Germans who
worked at Auschwitz were practicing Christians, and they
forced Jewish prisoners to sing "Silent Night."

*Caption: This room at
Auschwitz was the
"punishment" room.
Prisoners who disobeyed
the rules were sent there.*

Leave Us

Forget us
forget our generation
live like humans
forget us

we envied
plants and stones
we envied dogs

I'd rather be a rat
I told her then

I'd rather not be
I'd rather sleep
and wake up when war is over

Forget us
don't enquire about our youth
leave us

(*Leave Us* by Tadeusz Rözewicz. Quoted in
Hilda Schiff, *Holocaust Poetry*)

PEOPLE IN THE CAMPS

The Commandant

E ACH CAMP was overseen by a commandant. These SS officers were in charge of the daily life of the camp. Franz Stangl, the commandant of Sobibor and then Treblinka, was a practicing Catholic who considered himself a devoted family man. Finally tried and convicted of war crimes in 1970, Stangl lacked any sense of moral responsibility. "That was my profession," he stated. "I enjoyed it. It fulfilled me."

The commandant about whom the most is known is Rudolf Höss. After going into hiding after the war, Höss was captured, tried, and executed at Auschwitz in April 1947. After his arrest, Höss wrote an account of his time as Auschwitz's first commandant. Like Stangl, he showed a startling unawareness of his inhumanity. "I must emphasize here that I have never personally hated the Jews," he wrote. His memoir includes harrowing observations, like the fact that "women who either guessed or knew what awaited them nevertheless found

Above: Josef Kramer was an SS officer who served at Dachau, Sachsenhausen, Mauthausen, and Auschwitz before becoming commandant at Bergen-Belsen in the last months of the war.

Left: Camp commandants lived in comfortable accommodations, sometimes with their family, on or near the grounds of the camp. This was the house of the commandant of the Belzec death camp in Poland.

"I Deeply Regret"

My family, to be sure, were well provided for in Auschwitz. Every wish that my wife or children expressed was granted them. The children could live a free and untrammelled life. My wife's garden was a paradise of flowers . . . . No former prisoner can ever say that he was in any way or at any time badly treated in our house. My wife's greatest pleasure would have been to give a present to every prisoner who was in any way connected with our household.

...In summer they [his children] splashed in the paddling pool in the garden, or in the Sola. But their greatest joy was when Daddy bathed with them. He had, however, so little time for all these childish pleasures. Today I deeply regret that I did not devote more time to my family. I always felt I had to be on duty the whole time.

Rudolf Höss, commandant of Auschwitz, writing from a Polish prison after the war.

(Quoted in Jadwiga Bezwińska and Danuta Czech (eds), *KL Auschwitz*)

the courage to joke with the children to encourage them, despite the mortal terror visible in their own eyes."

Höss, like Stangl, was brought up in a religious family, and his parents wanted him to become a priest. But the young man joined the army when he was only 16 and took part in World War I. In the early 1920s he was sentenced to life imprisonment for involvement in a political murder, but he was freed after five years. Höss joined the SS, gained promotion after working at Dachau and Sachsenhausen, and was chosen by Himmler to be in charge of Auschwitz. He directed the expansion of the Auschwitz complex into Germany's largest concentration and death camp. With his wife and their five children, he lived at Auschwitz in a simple house separated from the rest of the camp by a concrete wall.

Above: The young Rudolph Höss, first commandant of Auschwitz. In captivity after the war, he wrote a memoir that tried to justify his actions.

The SS

The SS came into existence in 1923 as a group of bodyguards for Hitler. When Himmler took control of the group four years later, there were fewer than 300 members. Himmler conceived of the SS as an elite force of blond-haired, blue-eyed, racially superior Nazi "supermen." Clad in black uniforms with a frightening death's head insignia, the SS had become both the Nazi party police and an independent armed force of 250,000 men by the time the death camps began operation.

In common with many of those at the other death camps, many of the 3,000 or so members of the SS who were quartered at Auschwitz received extra rations for participating in the gassing operations. For many the real bonus was that their lives were not in any physical danger, unlike SS units assigned to active combat situations. For high-ranking officers there were many privileges.

Below: These SS men and police officials at Buchenwald in Germany had an easy life— extra rations, living close to home, and, unlike those sent to the Russian front, little chance of being killed in action.

Above: A Christmas celebration at the Sachsenhausen concentration camp, which was north of Berlin.

The Deciding Factor

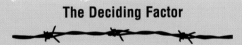

For Franz Hofmann, an SS member who served at Auschwitz, the decision to join the SS was one of practicality not morality:

I would also like to say that my decision to enter the SS was made easier by the fact that it did not cost me anything. My brother, who later died on the Eastern Front, had previously been a member of the SS until he was expelled for some reason, so I was able to have his uniform and did not have to buy myself a new one. I would like to say today that I would certainly not have become a member of the SS if I had not been able to use my brother's uniform. The uniform was the deciding factor.

(Quoted in E. Klee, W. Dressen & V. Riess, *Those Were the Days*)

Kapos and *Mussulmen*

Prisoners who survived the first selection process were destined for a grueling term of hard labor. The Germans organized the inmates' workload by using prisoners to oversee the system for them. The routine of daily life, like the lengthy morning roll call, was overseen by selected prisoners, known as *kapos* in camp jargon. They were responsible for day-to-day affairs. Kapos were usually non-Jewish Germans, either political prisoners or just criminals, and they answered to a small number of SS men. From a prisoner's point of view the kapos were powerful, and getting on the wrong side of them could spell disaster. One survivor called them the "aristocrats of the camps." Simple matters like the assignment of duties could be crucial. If a kapo could be bribed or persuaded to assign someone to indoor work, this might make the difference between life and death.

The kapos' privileged position meant they had their own rooms in the barracks, but the SS guards could always demote them at a moment's notice, and then they faced the wrathful revenge of the common prisoners.

While kapos were the most likely to survive in a camp, the least likely to survive were those whose strength of will gave way. In camp slang, these individuals were often referred to as Mussulmen, which means "Muslims." The term came from the mistaken idea that a Muslim's belief in fate meant a surrender of the will and a willingness to accept one's fate as inevitable. Mussulmen described those inmates who gave up believing they could survive, whose sense of self and will to live was crushed and broken, whose ordeal robbed them of any sense of control.

Opposite: Kapos faced the wrath of former prisoners after the liberation of the camps in 1945.

Below: Kapos, like the men seen here not wearing stripes, lived relatively privileged lives in the camps. They were usually German criminals rather than Jews.

Diary of an SS Officer

From the diary of Dr. Johann Paul Kramer, an SS officer who served at Auschwitz in 1942:

September 6: Today an excellent Sunday dinner: tomato soup, one half of chicken with potatoes and red cabbage, and magnificent vanilla ice cream.

September 20: This Sunday afternoon I listened from 3 pm till 6 pm to a concert of the prisoners' band in glorious sunshine; the bandmaster was a conductor of the State Opera from Warsaw. Eighty musicians. Roast pork for dinner . . .

September 27: This Sunday afternoon, from 4 till 8, a party in the club with supper, free beer, and cigarettes. Speech of Commandant Höss and a musical and theatrical program . . .

November 8: . . . We had Bulgarian red wine and plum brandy from Croatia.

(Quoted in E. Klee, W. Dressen & V. Riess, *Those Were the Days*)

The *Sonderkommando*

Sonderkommando (the word means "special command") was the term used for Jewish prisoners who had the most gruesome tasks in the death camps. Their job was to channel those selected for immediate death into the gas chambers with the minimum of fuss. They maintained the pretense that the prisoners were only being sent for a shower, advising them to undress and pack their clothes carefully so that they could be collected afterwards. A Jewish doctor at Auschwitz described how, opening the gas chamber doors afterward, the *Sonderkommando* stood equipped with their rubber boots and water hoses to wash down the bodies. After tying straps around the wrists of the corpses, they dragged them out and into a nearby room. This room led to the elevators that could carry more than 20 bodies to the crematorium.

Below at right: In September 1941, 33,771 Jews from Kiev were taken to a ravine outside the city of Babi Yar in the Ukraine and shot. The photo shows SS men picking through the victims' clothes.

Another *Sonderkommando* team waited to remove the bodies from the elevator and feed them into the giant ovens. First, they cut off and collected the hair of the victims and extracted any gold teeth. Sometimes people in the *Sonderkommando* team were selected because of their skills, like the dentists who were chosen for the task of extracting teeth from the dead prisoners.

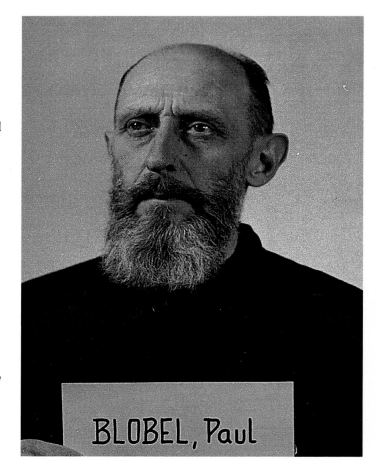

Right: Paul Blobel was the head of the SS team that carried out the executions at Babi Yar. He was sentenced to death at the War Crimes Trials in 1948.

BLOBEL, Paul

"The Competition"

I estimate that the number of Jews gassed at Sobibor was about 350,000. In the canteen at Sobibor I once overheard a conversation between Frenzel, Stangl, and Wagner. They were discussing the number of victims in the extermination camps of Belzec, Treblinka, and Sobibor and expressed their regret that Sobibor "came last" in the competition.

From a statement by Erich Bauer, a guard at Sobibor.
(Quoted in E. Klee, W. Dressen & V. Riess, *Those Were the Days*)

While they were alive, *Sonderkommando* in the camps enjoyed a better material standard of living than their fellow prisoners. One survivor has described how he arrived at the special barracks reserved for them and found a table laid for dinner with "fine initialed porcelain dishes, and place settings of silver" (stolen from the luggage of Jews). But the lifespan of a *Sonderkommando* was always brief, and in time most of them found themselves being shepherded into the gas chambers by those selected to replace them.

Doctors

Doctors were seldom needed at camps such as Sobibor and Chelmno, which were purely dedicated to exterminating Jews. But at Auschwitz they were employed to select those prisoners who seemed to be fit and healthy enough for slave labor.

Josef Mengele is the most infamous of the various doctors who used the death camps as laboratories for medical experiments—unhampered by any concept of legality or medical ethics. Any organization or company in Germany could make a request to the SS central office in Berlin for an experiment. For example, Bayer, the huge pharmaceutical company, requested that female prisoners be used to test a new drug. While working at Auschwitz

Below: An Auschwitz survivor receives treatment from a Russian doctor in January 1945.

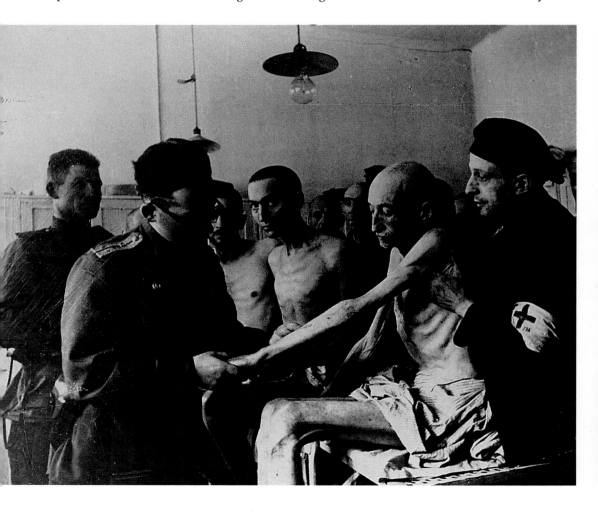

on a method of increasing the birth rate of Germans, Mengele became interested in the physical and genetic make-up of identical twins. So twins became some of the few children not immediately selected for death. Investigations into methods of sterilizing Jews and other "inferior" races led to experiments with radiation and injections of different formulas. Like Mengele's twins, victims who survived the experiments were usually gassed afterward. The results of some experiments were written up and presented as scientific papers to doctors at conferences in Germany.

Below: Josef Mengele, SS officer and doctor at Auschwitz between May 1943 and November 1944, murdered many Jews in the course of carrying out his brutal experiments.

"There was Nothing I Could Do"

Maximilian Grabner was an SS officer who helped administer the death camps. In a statement made after the war he explained his actions this way:

To kill three million people is in my view the greatest crime of all. I only took part in this crime because there was nothing I could do to change anything.... I am a Roman Catholic and today still believe in God. I believe there must be such a thing as divine justice as well as justice on Earth. I only took part in the murder of some three million people out of consideration for my family. I was never an anti-Semite and would still claim that every person has the right to life.

(Quoted in E. Klee, W. Dressen & V. Riess, *Those Were the Days*)

THE END OF THE CAMPS

The End of Belzec and Chelmno

B Y THE end of 1942, most of Poland's three million Jews had been exterminated. This meant that some of the death camps created mainly for this purpose were no longer needed or could slow down the pace of murder. In December 1942, Belzec camp became the first to close down its gas chambers. Auschwitz's size and efficiency made it sufficient to deal with the remaining Jews and other minorities who were to be wiped out.

The crematoriums at Belzec were dismantled, the buildings burned down and cleared away, and the remaining Jews shot. No trace remained of a camp where 600,000 people had been

Below: During the winter of 1942, the remaining Jewish prisoners at Belzec were shot. This woman waits to die.

murdered. By 1946, the year after World War II ended, there were only two survivors of Belzec alive. One of them, Chaim Hirszman, was giving evidence in the nearby town of Lublin when he was murdered by Poles on his way home—because he was a Jew.

Chelmno death camp did not begin to close down until the end of 1944. It took over two months for a remaining group of 100 Jews to dismantle the crematoriums. By the middle of January 1945 there were 41 left alive. They were then taken out of their barracks one night in groups of five and shot. One prisoner was shot but not killed. He managed to survive, as did another one who managed to stab an SS guard and escape into nearby woods.

Below: A German officer stands by a truck filled with corpses as a British news team records his explanation of what happened.

The Last March

Giza Landau was 13 when she arrived at Auschwitz in late 1944. She took part in the final forced evacuation of the camp:

The Russians must have been very close by then, as the Germans were in a great hurry. We were not allowed to stop even for a moment, day or night. If someone bent over to straighten their shoe or have a rest, or if someone grew weak and could not keep up, they were shot on the spot. We marched down side roads, through woods, in the snow. All along the way there were corpses, some of them even in a sitting position. I tried not to look but it was impossible to avoid them. After two days we were put in into open wagons. There was no food whatsoever; there was no more bread, and we ate snow. No one believed any longer that they would survive.

(Quoted in Maria Hochberg-Marianska and Noe Grüss (eds), *The Children Accuse*)

Killings and Uprisings

Even as it became clear that Germany's military defeat was only a matter of time, further executions were organized, apparently to kill as many Jews as possible before the end of the war. In less than one week in November 1943, 50,000 Jews were taken to Majdanek death camp and shot in front of ditches behind the gas chambers. At Auschwitz in 1944, even keeping the crematoriums burning 24 hours a day was not enough to keep up with the Nazis' determination to kill all of Hungary's Jews. Huge pits were dug in which as many as 2,000 bodies were burned together. The fires could be seen as far as 30 miles (48 km) away.

Near the end of the war, uprisings took place in various camps. In August 1943 at Treblinka, 150 Jews escaped, killing 15 of the guards, though some of them were hunted down and shot. In October, 300 prisoners escaped from Sobibor. Most were captured or killed. Three hundred more were killed trying to escape. In the same month the 700 *Sonderkommando* at Auschwitz rose in revolt, but nearly all were killed by the SS.

Below: After the Sobibor uprising in 1943, about 300 prisoners fled into the woods. It is thought that about 60 of them survived the war, including this group.

Above: The remains of part of the vast Auschwitz camp still stand as a reminder of what happened behind those barbed-wire fences.

"How Alive They Were"

Fania Fenelon was in Bergen-Belsen when Allied troops liberated the camp:

Our liberators were well fed and bursting with health, and they moved among our skeletal, tenuous silhouettes like a surge of life . . . . They called to one another, whistled cheerfully, then suddenly fell silent, faced with eyes too large, or too intense a gaze. How alive they were; they walked quickly, they ran, they leapt. All these movements were so easy for them, while a single one of them would have taken away our last breath of life! These men seemed not to know that one could live in slow motion, that energy was something you saved.

(Quoted in Martin Gilbert, *The Holocaust*)

Hiding the Evidence: Majdanek, Treblinka, and Auschwitz

With the Soviet advance westward in 1944, liberation of the death camps became inevitable. Himmler ordered the closedown of Majdanek and the evacuation of the remaining prisoners to Auschwitz, which was farther west. On July 24, 1944, a Polish resistance group took control of Majdanek. They greeted the Soviet troops when they arrived soon afterward.

In late 1943 Treblinka was dismantled. The remaining Jews were executed. So complete was the destruction of the camp that there was little left to indicate that 800,000 human beings had perished within its 60 acres (24 ha). Sobibor was physically dismantled in the same way, with little or no evidence left of what had happened there.

The last victims died at Auschwitz on October 28, 1944. Within a month, the dismantling of the machinery of mass murder and the destruction of written records of what had taken place was ordered. Meticulous records had been kept, right down to falsifying death certificates for those gassed. In January 1945, when Auschwitz was being evacuated, the Germans tried to burn down Canada, the barracks that held the prisoners' belongings, but not everything was destroyed. The Soviet soldiers who first arrived were astonished to find among the ruins vast quantities of belongings: nearly 14,000 rugs, 38,000 pairs of shoes,

Below: This young person entered Auschwitz some time during 1943. When the camps were closed, all records, including this one, were to be burned, but many of them survived.

350,000 men's suits, and hundreds of thousands of articles of women's clothing. Some of these items can be seen today at the museum at Auschwitz.

Left: This picture, called No Escape, *by Moshe Galili shows a German executioner along with American, British, and Russian soldiers. The painting implies that the Allies were guilty, too, for not preventing the Holocaust or for not stopping it sooner.*

Buchenwald

In April 1945, on the day that Buchenwald was liberated, the American correspondent Edward Murrow made a radio broadcast describing what he saw:

We went to the hospital. It was full. The doctor told me that 200 had died the day before. I asked the cause of death. He shrugged and said, "TB, starvation, fatigue, and there are many who have no desire to live."… [Another prisoner] showed me the daily ration: one piece of brown bread about as thick as your thumb, on top of it a piece of margarine as big as three sticks of chewing gum. That, and a little stew, was what they received every 24 hours.

(Quoted in Louis L. Snyder, *Encyclopedia of the Third Reich*)

The Death Marches

By the middle of 1944 the victorious Russians were advancing toward Germany, and the end of World War II in Europe was only a matter of time. In early 1945, the remaining prisoners were evacuated and forced to march out of the death and concentration camps of eastern Poland. The SS wanted a slave labor force to build their final defenses against the Allied armies. By January 1945 the Russians were close enough to Auschwitz to bombard parts of it with artillery, and the SS ordered the evacuation of the camp. The remaining Jews in Buchenwald were evacuated by the Germans in April. The injured and sick were left behind, and of the 60,000 who were marched off westward through the snow, about 20,000 died along the way. The camp was liberated a week later, on January 27, 1945. The Soviet soldiers found the thousands of near-dead prisoners who had been left behind.

About 10,000 of those who marched out of Auschwitz, along with thousands of others evacuated from other camps, ended up in Bergen-Belsen concentration camp in Germany. British soldiers and tanks entered the camp in April 1945, after the Germans had left, and found thousands of unburied bodies—those who had died of starvation. Bulldozers had to be brought in to help bury them. Three hundred continued to die each day for a week. One of those who died at Bergen-Belsen in the last weeks of the war was a young Jewish girl, Anne Frank, who had recorded her daily thoughts while hiding in a house in Amsterdam with her family, before her capture. After the war, her journal was published at *The Diary of a Young Girl*. It is one of the most famous pieces of Holocaust literature.

At Mauthausen, U.S. soldiers found thousands of starving prisoners near death. Many of them died in the following weeks.

Below: American soldiers look on in horror at the victims who died in the final weeks of the Holocaust.

"How Old Do You Think I Am?"

A middle-aged German woman approaches me.

"We didn't know anything. We had no idea. You must believe me. Did you have to work hard also?"

"Yes," I whisper.

"At your age, it must've been difficult." At my age. What does she mean?

"We didn't get enough to eat. Because of starvation. Not because of my age."

"I meant, it must have been harder for the older people." For older people?

"How old do you think I am?"

She looks at me uncertainly.

"Sixty? Sixty-two?"

"Sixty? I am fourteen. Fourteen years old."

She gives a little shriek and makes the sign of the cross. In horror and disbelief she walks away and joins the crowd of German civilians near the station house.

So this is liberation. It's come.

I am fourteen years old, and I have lived a thousand years.

(Quoted in Livia Bitton-Jackson, *I Have Lived a Thousand Years*)

The Germans surrendered to the Allies in May 1945, but thousands of camp prisoners died for many weeks afterwards. Their body weight reduced to less than 66 lb. (30 kg), approximately the weight of a 7-year-old child, they had no strength or will left to live. Those who did recover their health would be haunted by what they had lived through.

Above: By April 1945, the German concentration camps were being evacuated. These prisoners from Dachau are being forced to march to an unknown destination.

DATELINE

1933 **January** Hitler appointed chancellor of Germany
March First concentration camp set up at Dachau

1935 **September** New laws remove Jewish legal rights and forbid marriage between Jews and non-Jews

1937 **September** Buchenwald concentration camp is established in Germany

1939 **September** Start of World War II
November All Jews in Nazi-occupied Europe made to wear a yellow Star of David
December All Jewish males between 14 and 60 are designated for forced labor in labor camps that are established throughout Poland

1940 **October** The deportation of Jews to the Warsaw ghetto begins

1941 **June** Germany invades Russia
September Experiments with gassing prisoners begin at Auschwitz
October Deportation of Jews to eastern Poland begins
December First Jews gassed at Chelmno

1942 **January** Wannsee Conference confirms arrangements for the Final Solution
March to October Deportation of Jews from France and Norway begins
March The first transports of Jews to Belzec, Majdanek, Sobibor, and Treblinka get under way
May Start of large-scale gassings at Auschwitz
September Start of large-scale gassings at Majdanek

1943 **January** Germans surrender at Stalingrad in Russia
April End of gassings at Chelmno
August End of gassings at Treblinka
October After the Nazi occupation of northern Italy, Italian Jews are deported to Auschwitz

1944 **May** Start of deportations of Hungarian Jews to Auschwitz
June Russians advancing westward; D-Day: Allies land in northern France; Start of death marches
July Polish resistance take control of Majdanek, and Soviet forces enter the camp
October Last victim gassed at Auschwitz

1945 **January** Evacuation of remaining prisoners from Auschwitz; Auschwitz liberated by Russians
April Bergen-Belsen and Buchenwald liberated by Allies
May Germany surrenders to Allies

RESOURCES

FURTHER READING AND SOURCES

Bauer, Yehuda. *History of the Holocaust.* Danbury, CT: Franklin Watts, 1992.

Dawidowicz, Lucy. *The War Against the Jews.* New York: Penguin, 1990.

Frank, Anne. *The Diary of Anne Frank.* New York: Bantam, 1993.

Friedlander, Saul. *Nazi Germany and the Jews: The Years of Persecution 1933-1939.* New York: HarperCollins, 1998.

Gilbert, Martin. *The Holocaust.* New York: Henry Holt, 1987.

Grant, R. G. *The Holocaust: New Perspectives.* New York: Raintree Steck-Vaughn, 1998.

Gutman, Israel. *Resistance: The Warsaw Ghetto Uprising.* New York: Houghton-Mifflin, 1997.

Hilberg, Raul. *The Destruction of the European Jews.* Holmes and Meier, 1985.

Keneally, Thomas. *Schindler's List.* Touchstone, 1993.

Laquer, Walter (ed). *The Holocaust Encyclopedia.* New Haven, CT: Yale University Press, 2001.

Levi, Primo. *Survival in Auschwitz.* New York: Simon and Schuster, 1996.

Rohrlich, Ruby (ed.) *Resisting the Holocaust.* New York: Berg, 1998.

Wiesel, Elie. *Night.* New York: Bantam, 1982.

INTERNET SITES

Shoah Visual History Foundation
www.vhf.org
Photographs and stories by survivors.

United States Holocaust Memorial Museum
www.ushmn.org
Pictorial history of the Holocaust

Yad Veshem
www.yad-vashem.org
Official website for the Holocaust Martyrs' and Heroes' Remembrance Authority

FILMS

The following movies are available to rent as videos or DVDs:

Schindler's List. Directed by Steven Spielberg from the book by Thomas Keneally, this is the story of a German factory owner who saved more than 1,000 Jews.

Shoah. Directed by Claude Lanzmann, this is a nine-hour documentary consisting entirely of interviews with survivors of and participants in the Holocaust.

Life is Beautiful. Directed by and starring Roberto Benigni, this controversial, Academy Award-winning film tells the fictional tale of an Italian Jewish father who creates a kind of make-believe contest out of the Nazi occupation in order to shelter his son from the horrors of the Holocaust.

PLACES TO VISIT

United States Holocaust Memorial Museum
100 Raoul Wallenberg Place SW
Washington, D.C. 20024
Phone: (202) 488-0400
Website: www.ushm.org
Library: library@ushm.org
(202) 479-9717

GLOSSARY

Allies countries that fought in World War II against Germany, Japan, and their allies; the Allies were the United States, Great Britain, the Soviet Union, and France.

Anti-Semitism prejudice against Jewish people.

Auschwitz the largest death camp in Poland, first established in 1941 as a prison labor camp.

Belzec a death camp in Poland that used gas chambers to murder about 600,000 Polish Jews.

Buchenwald concentration camp established in Germany in 1938.

Chelmno death camp, established in western Poland at the end of 1941, that used gas vans to kill some 400,000 Jews who were deported there.

Communism the theory that all property should be collectively owned.

Concentration camps large-scale prison and work camps, where prisoners were often worked to death but not in the systematic manner of the death camps.

Crematoriums places where corpses are disposed of by burning.

Dachau the first Nazi concentration camp, established in March 1933 and liberated by American troops in April 1945.

Death camps also known as extermination camps, dedicated to systematically murdering their inmates, mostly Jews. The six Nazi death camps were in Poland: Auschwitz, Belzec, Chelmno, Majdanek, Sobibor, and Treblinka.

Death marches the forced evacuation of camp prisoners during the last stages of the war. Many thousands of the prisoners died or were murdered on these marches.

Deportation to remove people by force to another country, as in the Nazi deportations of Jews from their homes to death, concentration, and labor camps in Poland.

Einsatzgruppen special Nazi units ordered to eliminate enemies of the state, responsible for the mass killing of Jews and communists in occupied Poland and Russia.

Extermination complete destruction (of a race or species).

Final Solution from the Nazi term *Endlösung*. The phrase "Final Solution of the Jewish Question" was used when referring to the extermination of all European Jews.

Führer the German word for "leader," the title assumed by Hitler in 1934.

Genocide deliberate destruction of a racial, religious, political, or ethnic group.

Ghettos districts in European towns where Jews were forced to live by the Nazis.

Holocaust term used since World War II to refer to the murder of some six million Jews by the Nazis and their allies during World War II.

Kapos selected prisoners, put in charge of ordinary prisoners, who managed many of the daily routines of camp life.

Labor camps camps that used slave labor, mostly prisoners of war and Jews, to increase Germany's wartime production.

Majdanek one of the six Nazi death camps in Poland.

Mauthausen a concentration camp established in Austria before war broke out in 1939. Prisoners at Mauthausen were used as slave labor for nearby granite quarries that were owned by the SS.

Mussulmen camp jargon used by prisoners to describe others who had lost the will to survive.

Nazi Party (Nationalsozialistische Deutsche Arbeiterpartei) in English "National Socialist German Workers' Party." Led by Hitler, the Nazi party governed Germany between 1933 and 1945.

Shoah Hebrew term for the Holocaust.

Sobibor a death camp in Poland that began operation in April 1942.

SS (Schutzstaffel) in English "protection squads." Originally used as bodyguards to protect senior members of the Nazi Party, the SS developed into its most powerful organization, responsible for controlling the concentration and death camps.

Sonderkommando in the camps, a group of prisoners responsible for working the gas chambers and crematoriums.

Treblinka a death camp established in Poland in 1942.

Wannsee Conference a meeting of important Nazi leaders and officials that took place outside of Berlin at Lake Wannsee in January 1942. At the meetings, plans for the final solution were transmitted and finalized.

INDEX

Amery, Jean 37
Amsterdam 8
Auschwitz 6, 10, 11, 13, 14,
    16-19, 20, 21, 22, 24-25,
    27, 32-33, 34, 36, 39, 40
    41, 42, 43, 44, 48, 50, 52,
    54, 56, 58
    See also Birkenau

Babi Yar 48
Bauer, Erich 49
Bayer 50
Belzec 10, 11, 14, 15, 21, 52
Bergen-Belsen 15, 39, 42,
    55, 58
Birkenau 17
Blobel, Paul 48
Buchenwald 12, 20, 28, 40,
    44, 57, 58

Chelmno 10, 11, 14, 22, 34,
    50, 53
concentration camps 4, 6
    See also names of
    specific camps

Dachau 11, 20, 21, 37, 43,
    59
Death camps 6, 10, 13
    See also names of
    specific camps
Diary of a Young Girl (Frank),
    58

Eichmann, Adolf 30
Einsatzgruppen 7

Fenelon, Fania 55

Frank, Anne 58
Friedmann, Elli 35

Galili, Moshe 57
ghettoes 8, 9, 11, 34
Goebbels Joseph, 6, 9
Goldhagen Daniel, 19
Grabner Maximilian, 51
Gypsies 24

Himmler, Heinrich 8, 12, 16,
    18, 19, 22-23, 44, 56
Hirzman, Chaim 53
Hitler, Adolf 4, 9
Hitler's Willing Executioners
    (Goldhagen) 19
Hofmann, Franz 45
Hoss, Rudolf 16, 19, 22, 23,
    25, 42, 43
Hungary 30-31, 54

I.G. Farben 16, 17, 18, 20

kapos 8, 46
Kiev 48
Kramer, Johann Paul 47
Kramer, Josef 42
Kretschmer, Karl 9

Landau, Giza 53
Levi, Primo 33, 35
Lodz 14
Lublin 14

Majdanek 10, 13, 14, 15,
    54, 56
Mauthausen 6, 7, 12, 59
Mengele, Josef 50-51

Mentz, Will 29
Minsk 8
Mobius, Kurt 21
Murrow, Edward 57
Mussulmen 46

National German Socialist
    Worker's Party 4-5
Nazis *See* National German
    Socialist Worker's Party
Netherlands 5
No Escape 57

Poland 6, 11

Sachsenhausen 12, 34, 38,
    43, 45
Sacks, W. J. 7
selections 24-25, 32-33, 35,
    36-37
Sobibor, 10, 15, 21, 26, 42,
    49, 50, 54, 56
Shoah (film) 15, 28, 29
Sonderkommando 48-49, 54
Soviet Union 5, 7, 11, 30, 56
SS 6, 8, 9, 12, 26, 32, 40,
    44-47, 50, 51, 58
Stangl, Franz 42, 43, 49
Suchomel, Franz 15

Treblinka 10, 14, 15, 21, 26,
    27, 29, 42, 54, 56

Wannsee Conference 9
Warsaw 8

Zyklon B, 9, 20, 23